# P.S.1 SYMPOSIUM:
# A PRACTICAL AVANT-GARDE

**n+1 RESEARCH BRANCH PAMPHLET SERIES #1**

Mark Greif

Eliza Newman-Saul

Dushko Petrovich

Moderated by Keith Gessen

Transcribed by Alexandra Heifetz

2006, n+1 Research

# INTRODUCTION

**H**I. THANK YOU FOR COMING. I'm Keith Gessen, one of the editors of *n+1*.

One of the things that we expected to happen when we started a magazine that published fiction, and that didn't happen—one of the many things—is that people would bombard us with weird stuff they'd written. We expected stories that didn't make any sense, edible stories, or stories that caused you to go blind as you read them, and—it's good that this didn't happen. But it's also a little puzzling.

It may be our own fault. We've occasionally received stories that were not strictly traditional, and yet it seems that every time we do, one of the editors, or many of the editors, finds the story "derivative." It's the sort of word that conservative critics often use against anything that seems new to them—they say it's all been done before. So one knows that this is something conservatives say. And yet one feels what one feels.

So we're very pleased to have an opportunity to pursue in public a conversation we've been having among ourselves—about what actually *would* constitute something genuinely new, something genuinely progressive, and whether this thing would once again be called "avant-garde," or whether it would need to have some different name and different approach in order to be anything more than a ready-made museum piece. It's also an open question, for us, whether we *want* to be avant-garde, at this point.

The three speakers today begin with Mark Greif, who's one of the founding editors of *n+1*. He is the author of "Against Exercise," "The Concept of Experience," and "Radiohead, or the Philosophy of Pop." I want to read you part of something that Mark wrote in the first issue. This was about *McSweeney's*, a magazine that we have distinguished ourselves from in various ways. Mark argued that "the Eggersards," as he called them, were a "regressive avant-garde" that had emptied the typographical and tonal innovations of the avant-garde of "their classic interest in a search for truth."

> "Here is a drawing of a stapler," Eggers wrote under a drawing of a stapler in *A Heartbreaking Work*. An allusion to the best-known work of a second-rate surrealism,

Magritte's "Ceci n'est pas une pipe." But the gap
between word and picture is eliminated, a sexual
connotation is erased. The joke becomes absurdist
in the degraded sense, that is, pointless, and this
proves to be the Eggersard touch. Rejecting the new,
and the true, Eggersards attacked the avant-garde
hope for any transcendence of present conditions.

("The Intellectual Situation," *n+1* Number One)

So we've been fairly effective, in other words, at call-
ing out people who we thought were not genuinely
avant-garde, who had founded degraded or politically
or aesthetically misdirected avant-gardes. What we'd
like to do today is articulate what we actually would
want; what a transcendence of present conditions
would look like. Mark will be speaking for a progressive avant-garde.

The second speaker will be Dushko Petrovich,
who is the *n+1* art criticizer, as we call him. Dushko
has written for the magazine about Philip Guston and
El Greco at the Met, David Hockney and Amy Sillman at the Whitney; the art of graphic novels; and,
for the website, he has organized groups of pieces on
Ed Ruscha, Marvin Gates, and Steve Mumford. He is
also a painter, often in bright colors. Dushko will be
speaking for a practical avant-garde.

The third speaker is Eliza Newman-Saul, an
artist who lives in Brooklyn. Eliza's work is difficult

to describe. Right now she's working on a project on darkness, in which people are taken into the dark and interviewed about their experience of the dark, what the dark is like—and this is recorded in various ways. Eliza is going to give us propositions for the radical imagination.

So let's get to it. I will be encouraging questions afterward. Please think of some.

# AVANT-GARDE AND PROGRESSIVE

I DON'T HAVE MUCH TIME, so let me make my claim right away. I think when you look at the significance of the avant-garde, you can never just look at the avant-garde. A worthwhile avant-garde only comes into being in a field of art or intellect that keeps three distinct levels of values. One level is that of an everyday, ordinary, teachable, "neutral" practice that people still take seriously and genuinely like. In literature, we have the realistic novel about family life. In painting, a representational portrait or landscape. In intellect, explication of a text or a history of its creation. I'd call this level "academic," but I know that's confusing. You could also call it—drawing a term from Benjamin Kunkel's contribution to the *n+1* Number Four symposium on writing—the "perennial."

The avant-garde is then a distinct level of value that needs this academic or perennial level in order to make sense. Only with a robust perennial art beneath it can an avant-garde change an art's direction. Only thus does the avant-garde have a base of ordinary practice to kick against. Only thus is anything at stake.

But the other necessary level is the one that sometimes gets forgotten in discussions for and against the avant-garde. It intervenes between these two—the avant-garde and perennial—and is necessary, so to speak, for ever having allowed the avant-garde to rise up out of the ordinary in the first place. This level is the progressive. It's simply the idea of progress that exists in a field of art—or, sometimes, doesn't; progress not just for its own sake but because the form is getting better at something. Ultimately, the great avant-gardes survive and serve a purpose if they in part change the direction of daily practice, and in part get absorbed by daily practice to make its resources more comprehensive. It is only through the belief in progress that this interaction can occur.

Let me say something about *n+1*. One of the facts about avant-gardes is that they have a history of starting around little magazines. So if you get a group together, and you have a magazine, and a vision, and a manifesto, does that mean you have a will to produce an avant-garde? I think for *n+1* the will is not to constitute an avant-garde, though the other editors may disagree. That's not our job. The task is to restore the level of progress: the values and impetus that keep avant-garde practice from going about rootless and unanchored, and that keep the "perennial" from sinking into the swamp of itself, where it becomes fossilized.

°   °   °

Avant-garde, of course, is a military term, a detachment up front that leads the main body of troops and makes sure the way is clear for them to keep moving forward. But it has also meant a renewal or overthrowing of art: by new techniques, by a change in subject matter, and often by a deliberately offensive philosophy of life. We have the term in French because over the course of the late 19th and early 20th centuries artistic life in Paris came to be organized into tiny rival groups, which issued manifestos and started magazines and exhibitions in two arts, literature and painting. This reached its European apex after World War I, in various destructive purgations and literary revolutions. So when people talk about the historic avant-gardes, they talk about things like Dada, surrealism, futurism, imagism, vorticism, and secondarily about the earlier Parnassians, realists, symbolists, naturalists, and decadents. In the United States, the last avant-garde flowerings that everybody seems to agree on date to the 1940s through the 1960s. The high-end ones are associated with the Black Mountain School for poets, dancers, musicians, et cetera—people like Charles Olson, Merce Cunningham, John Cage—as well as the Abstract Expressionist painters. And then you start to get the arguable cases: a whole list of little schools, of Happenings and Situationism and Fluxus; San Francisco Renaissance, Beat, and New York School poets, et cetera. At this point the debate really devolves. The question becomes: Does this person qualify? And does that person qualify? How about the 1970s? How about the 1980s? It's like a child negotiating for an extra hour before bedtime. This is the miserable part of discussing the avant-gardes. Those petty discriminations make you want to give up.

◦  ◦  ◦

So although it is made by groups and manifestos and individuals, I would like to think of the avant-garde primarily as a functional level within any given art or field of intellect. And without asking who is most avant-garde, you can figure out whether a fruitful avant-garde exists by looking to see if it has a serious relation to levels below it.

It seems from the outside that the visual arts have an avant-garde problem. It sometimes seems that late-20th-century developments in the visual arts led to a situation in which only the avant-garde impulse is respected. The perennial or academy practice—straightforward portraits, harborside scenes, unironized history—has been exiled from the museum after the triumph of the modern. But the progressive belief in getting better depictions, truer to our changing subjectivity (an assumption which was central to early modernism) has been sidelined and demoted as somehow tyrannical. It looks from the outside as if this has led to a situation in which each new young artist who wants access to the museum is obliged to come up with a wholly novel and destructive idiom in which to revolutionize and overthrow the whole of art, or else find a tiny niche in someone else's overthrowing. When everyone promises to overthrow everything else, you find that none of the individuals can rationally believe they'll overthrow anything, and so visual art develops an odd weightlessness and comes to look more like ornament or anecdote.

Fiction is somewhat the reverse. There you have an incredibly strong and predominant "perennial" practice, in part because fiction remains commercial and popular. People write stories about "what happened to me and could happen to you" or "wouldn't it be strange if." They use an idiom that crosses traditional realism with technically conservative American modernisms from Hemingway, Faulkner, and an Americanized Kafka; or the first-person voice of the unreliable narrator. And fine—I like reading some of those things. There is a certain kind of experimental practice—sometimes it feels a little avant-garde, sometimes a little progressive—but often it just seems to be perennial work with gimmicky typography or spacing borrowed from the early-20th-century avant-gardes. In fiction you have all three levels, perhaps, but really mostly a bottom level—the perennial—which kids itself that it is also doing the job of the top two, while the top two are weak and demoralized.

Poetry, it sometimes seems, is more at risk of falling into the situation of the visual arts; that is, fragmenting into a crowd of weightless avant-gardes, with the absence of a progressive belief to make sense of experimental effort. On the plus side, poetry does have the strong presence of a "perennial" practice too: short unrhymed free verse lyrics about nature or people the poet is friends with or sees at the movies. It is a perennial practice, however, that was transformed by the techniques and freedoms of modernism—whether by Wallace Stevens, William Carlos Williams, or T. S. Eliot—without maintaining their programs of values (which would be museum pieces today). And so this perennial practice, except in its most conservative variants, seems confused and resentful about what it means and where it stands, or why it even uses the techniques it does.

Thus among the visual arts and literary arts you begin to see a certain see-saw of possibilities. Either there are fields which became overconvinced of their revolutionary and overthrowing character—and this may be associated, as chicken or egg, with a withdrawal from commercial popularity. Or there are fields which were overstabilized by commercial forces, as in the novel, because of the enormous rewards for perennial work or for an avant-garde which is really just the perennial wearing a hat. In both cases, this tilting to one side or the other occurs precisely because of the lost connection of progress.

∘ ∘ ∘

If there's any point at which my insistence on the progressive will be most frustrating to people, it's with the idea that progress in the arts means getting better at anything. How can art be progressive, in this sense, rather than just changeable—more like fashion, or "history"? What could be "better" in a history of undirected, contingent change?

I think the way in which the progressive arts and intellect do progress is by trying to give better and better accounts of the way in which our social reality changes—contingently, yes, but also chronologically and cumulatively. Not only is a long highway drive today not like riding in a horse-drawn carriage, it's not like a drive twenty-five years ago. Earlier modernism taught us to put into words or pictures what a lot of modern life felt like, but the thing is, there are constantly new daily phenomena that feel like something, and yet you can barely describe to yourself what they feel like. The progressive arts quite deliberately aim at moving targets, as opposed to perennial arts which shoot for stationary things that are already identified; or the sorts of avant-gardes that just get interested in their own guns or bows and arrows and don't shoot at anything, at least not to hit it.

It may be that the most useful avant-garde efforts right now are not those that are self-conscious about being avant-garde, but those that are most self-consciously able to render the symptoms of a reality that is changing elsewhere. This symptomatic practice of art puts together the progressive impulse to describe things better with the avant-garde impulse to fashion new techniques for the absolutely new. To take those things that make victims or demigods of us all, and yet are unarticulable by us, and to figure out how to picture them truly, or put them into new words, would be an art worth the trouble.

# FOR A PRACTICAL AVANT-GARDE

T HE AVANT-GARDE isn't what it used to be. Our sprawling culture industry busies itself mainly in locating things in the network presented by the relatively recent past. Everybody is described as the love child of so-and-so and so-and-so, so everybody gets called neo this or neo that, unless the parents are divorced—then they get called post. Not that we need a new "ism" exactly, but, ironically, looking back has gotten old.

Artists, in the meantime, have gotten young. They are being sold so young that they have to come with papers to confirm their lineage. Legions of culture workers produce wall paragraphs, catalogs, and magazine blurbs to confirm young debutantes. Collectors are thus invited to speculate on promising futures, but the art objects themselves look remarkably retro.

The big books about the avant-garde are also retrospective. Renato Poggioli gave us *The Theory of the Avant-Garde*, which is a dry book about the Romantics, and Rosalind Krauss wrote a book to show that the avant-garde was a modernist myth.* I am tempted to say that the post-avant-garde is then a postmodernist myth, but I'm not here to argue theory.

I am a painter, so I want to be practical about the situation. The various accounts of our condition that I have read have struck me as either hysterically reactionary or irresponsibly giddy. People decide that art is either dead or immortal, but no one wants to admit that it might be a little sick.

To remedy the situation, I am going to take a very simple position on the avant-garde. I stole it from Fairfield Porter, who said the avant-garde was always just the people with the most energy. The question for us is what should these energetic people do now? How should we advance?

To answer this question, I am going to talk about rectangles.

As the last century thought more and more about painting, it produced more and more plain rectangles. They came in different national flavors. In Russia, Malevich's squares were hung high in the room and compared to icons and revolutions. In the European

---

* Rosalind E. Krauss, *The Originality of the Avant-Garde and Other Modernist Myths*. MIT Press: 1985.

North, the rectangles were cold and got turned into furniture. When Mondrian brought them to New York, they got jazzy. In America, we had the great rigid aphorisms of Ad Reinhardt, and his black rectangles ended painting. But painting kept ending, so by the '70s we got Mel Bochner's various conceptual grey grids, followed by Peter Halley's more up-to-date day-glo rectangles. Then Halley went on to found a magazine and run a grad school, and here we are.

Paintings, apart from the very occasional tondo or altarpiece triangle, all start out as rectangles. But to end up with just a rectangle, you have to keep a whole lot of things out. This repudiation, too, comes in different flavors. You could reject the tsarist system, transcend all representational antics, or just have your studio assistants get out the masking tape and go to town. Photography, or revolution, or atomic weapons had repeatedly pushed painting into a zone of near-paralytic self-consciousness. By the late '50s, flatness was enthroned, with zip lines and stripes providing the only variation. Everything—the body, gesture, ideas, materials, politics, process, and critical dialogue—was taken out of paintings to make them correct and serene. That was the avant-garde of the rectangle.

Its impolite rival and savior is now called post-minimalism, but it went by many names: body art, performance art, conceptual art, land art, protest art, process art, anti-art art. Ana Mendieta rolled in mud.

Vito Acconci, now an architect, sat under a slanted gallery floor and masturbated for days on end. Chris Burden nailed himself to a Volkswagen, was shot in the arm, and shot at airplanes with real bullets. Not having been there, we learn about these new art forms from the leftover paraphernalia. Books and museums show us black and white photographs, gallery invites, artists' statements and manifestos—all of minimal visual interest—and the putatively unrectangular event gets reduced, through a ruse of history, into that very familiar rectangle: the 8 ½ by 11 sheet of copy paper in a course packet.

Minimalism and postminimalism agreed on one thing: eliminate pictures. Painting took to a pure territory, while the new art forms expanded the realm of art to every conceivable issue and strategy. The scene seemed wild, but there were simple rules all along. You were given a white room in a Big Art City for a month. You had to do something in that room to generate attention beyond that month. You had to be written about, bought, or at least widely discussed. Then you would get to have the white room again for another month, and so on. If you did this enough, you had what was called a career. This generated what is perhaps this century's biggest art movement: careerism.

But back to our schematic. This white room of the gallery was really a box, so the avant-garde of the rectangle led in a strange way to the avant-garde of the box. And a box with things in it is pretty much a picture, which is weird because the picture, you remember, had been eliminated.

But nevermind, because the whole thing worked out very well: these days, it is hard to find people who don't feel a direct and lively connection to contemporary art. We download inspiring artists' statements and argue passionately in front of wall paragraphs. We are improved by repeated confrontations with oblique titles, obscure maps, and obsessive doodles. The rigorous inspection of art objects has armed us against the ruses of late capitalism, and our political art unites us in struggle. Strict formalism, for its part, has given museum visitors a sense of deep spirituality. When we see the grids of rocks in stark rooms, we are moved. Our eyes are soft from weeping.

Just kidding. Actually, I think the game in the box has gotten the best of us. Almost everyone would agree that the art world has become a kind of spectacle. I also might not be alone in finding much of the work repetitive and derivative in a way that starts to resemble planned cultural obsolescence. We have been forced to endure neo-expressionism, neo-cubism, neo-geo, neo-minimalism, and neo-Dada, all under the law of diminishing returns. This strange cycle has set in due largely to the game in the box, whereby the most valuable attribute an artist can have is promise. With

18

a lot of big bets being placed, the artist has to be both young and verifiable. In other words, marketable. But almost none of our superstar artists have delivered on their promise. The big investments from the last art boom in the '80s, for example, have not matured in any sense of the word. Like the society at large, the art world is turning into teenagers and aging teenagers.

To really grow up, we have to be able to decide what is really good. Art world insiders have trends but few criteria. The word they most often use to describe art is "interesting." Reactionaries have criteria, but no art. Their favorite art word is "bad." So the people with the most energy, a.k.a. the avant-garde, have a particular responsibility in this kind of situation. They have to find a way to use the word "good." After that, we can talk again about something being great.

I am a painter, so I am going to speak to the situation in painting, but this specialized speech is actually against specialization, so I hope it can be useful to other disciplines.

First of all, as an avant-garde, we have to be willing to say goodbye to the plain rectangles and to the game in the box. We do this by bringing them together. Painting is, miraculously, both a rectangle and a box. It is pure and still, but at the same time, it can hold anything. Great painting has always been incredibly formal and incredibly involved in the world. For hundreds and even thousands of years, it has been technically advanced, formal, and self-aware while at the same time being conceptual, bodily, political, performative, religious, profane, seductive, and satiric. There was no need, in other words, to break up the party.

As painters invite back all that was banished—sunsets, flowers, history, philosophy, the body—they have a responsibility to painting's special powers. Painting is, I think we can now admit, a very effective way to play the game of the box and the rectangle. A good painting does this by simultaneously holding both objects from the world and our attention. Unlike the gallery box, a good painting does not disintegrate after a month. Some have held our attention for hundreds of years. A good painting also does not depend on textual support and can thus cross national and linguistic borders and communicate over time. In a word, good paintings are autonomous.

Therefore, a practical avant-garde should measure itself. It should not wait for schools, publications, galleries, or even museums to measure it.

A practical avant-garde is post-careerist. It seeks out low rent and private time, and it concentrates on powerful objects.

A practical avant-garde experiments, but is honest about the results, displaying only the work that is full-fledged and generous. It surveys past achievements with similar honesty, looking at past experiments with an eye for what was deep. We can see, for example, that in addition to the avant-garde that ended in plain rectangles and new art movements, there were many other avant-gardes. The avant-garde of the surface of the painting would include people like Pierre Bonnard, Georges Braque, and Robert Ryman. A narrative avant-garde would include people like Max Beckmann, Stanley Spencer, Jacob Lawrence, and, more recently, William Kentridge. Aristocratic pranksters like Marcel Duchamp and Balthus unwittingly constitute another avant-garde, expanding the kinds of attitudes one can take toward the art world, and toward painting.

The practical avant-garde knows the difference between a picture and an image. It knows that images are ubiquitous and coercive, while real pictures are rare. A practical avant-garde can build on the recent achievements of radical picture-makers like Philip Guston, Ed Ruscha, Amy Sillman, Neo Rauch, and Peter Doig. It has to take the minor achievements of many other artists and synthesize them into a powerful picture.

The practical avant-garde has a lot of work to do. It knows that manifesto is the weakest genre and that promises are irrelevant, so it will use words but not hide behind them. Finally, the practical avant-garde is grateful to the impractical avant-garde, but we will not defer to it.

THERE ARE THOSE OF US who don't fit in, those of us who could never quite pull it off, who brought gefilte fish for lunch to a Christian elementary school and were teased for years. There are subcultures decked out in black nail polish and fetishists with stuffed animals strapped to their dicks, and there are categories like "avant-garde" to explain our tendencies. I remember the first time I heard anyone say "avant-garde." It was my great-aunt in New York City trying to explain to my grandparents that this friend of theirs was gay. "He's very, um, avant-garde."

Once, in history, there was an avant-garde, and then, in later history, there was a neo-avant-garde, which I will leave to Benjamin Buchloh to define, and then after that there were kids trying to explain why they didn't fit in in high school, and they were the new neo-almost-nervous avant-garde.

I don't really want to talk about this label in particular; rather, I want to talk about a mode of thinking that is associated with the avant-garde, a way of thinking that is fundamentally a refusal. It links back to a sorrow associated with the tragedy of war, a fundamental despair that permeates those who doubt the world, those who want things to change, those who are desperate for change and a chance to start over.

Years after the gefilte fish disaster, I was walking out of high school in a ball gown, gloves, and with wings attached to my shoes when Joe Gonzalez, a truly committed crusty punk, started chatting with me. He never took a shower. Joe never took a shower to the point that he was suspended from school for smelling so bad. He had on bondage pants and a Black Flag T-shirt—really the only clothes he ever wore in the four years that I knew him. We were talking about

my brother or something light when he turned to me
and said,

And I thought to myself, "*I'm* weird! *I'm* weird! Listen,
stinky . . ."

o   o   o

The body in extreme pain disassociates, separates
from reality, and hallucination sets in. I should note
that I am skeptical of the term "hallucination" because
it is too bodily a diagnosis, so perhaps we could describe this experience as a de-identification or disas-

sociation which allows for imagination to set in. This form of protest—rejecting reality and protecting oneself against reality—led me to found the Institute for the Return of the Radical Imagination. It was my attempt to justify the necessity of the imagination in art, life, politics, or whatever your poison may be. I doubted the power or political relevance of protest. "I don't believe that conventional forms of protest can really change anything," I would explain to friends or unfortunate bus passengers. The act of placing your body in the way, of taking up space as a form of revolt, no longer seems relevant. We are post-body. The image is just as manipulable as the mind. You can make anything disappear. We are in an age of hiding, of nostalgia, of research, and re-imagination.

When I was young, in my winged shoes and fancy dresses, I looked for those models in continental literature and Russian politics. I entered my own age of research. I read to the point that my parents became nervous that I was agoraphobic and tried to pay me to leave the house. And instead of falling in love with Scott Gilmore, whom I passed in the halls, I developed crushes on Apollinaire, Mallarmé, and Trotsky, and I would write them love letters:

Dear Guilliame,

I am imagining language in the shape of your body, in the shape of our bodies pressed languidly together, words forming desire between us.

When it rains I can only think of you.

Love,

Eliza

And when Scott Gilmore did finally weasel his way into my house, when I did finally kiss him in the attic,

Scott Gilmore

on the dusty floor, my mind drifted to Trotsky and I wrote in my notebook that night:

> I don't know how to believe in change because I have been told that change is a fiction. I love fictions and doubt the "real." I have been told that fiction and fantasy are reactionary, self-revelatory, and masturbatory. The first time I kissed a boy I thought of Trotsky. I need fantasy to be involved in the world. My fantasies are more involved in the world than I am. Though I keep returning to the fantasy

of solution, I cannot solve anything. All I can do is
coordinate.

Naming yourself, aligning yourself with a certain
historical moment, is an attempt to create a community, to coordinate. Blanchot describes surrealism
as instituting a collective experience, and he admires
Breton for his capability not to be "the *one* any more
than the others, but of making surrealism each one's
Other." He describes this as a form of "friendship in
the most rigorous sense of this exacting term: that is,
making the surrealist affirmation, in other words, a
presence of a work of friendship." What I didn't understand in my ball gown and winged shoes standing next
to Punk Rock Joe was that he was participating in a
community, perhaps an Other's other community in a
realm like high school, but an established world none-
theless. Joe's freakish, disruptive dress was historically
relevant and useful while my dress was strange; it was
not "punk rock." His clothes excluded some but also
signaled to other punks who he was. I, on the other
hand, was imagining myself as part of a community
that had no concrete possibilities for friendship or
collective experience. It was an imagined community based on books and photographs. I was isolating
myself in my mind. And, instead of having friends, I
imagined places like Swann's Way, like Durrell's Alex-
andria, and, later, FOOD or the Cedar Tavern where

I had heard that this community existed; these spots where the world existed through them, around them. I imagined architecture as a third figure in a romance. And I imagined going to parties with smiling faces, and warm hellos, where revolutionaries would kiss artists. Where the avant-garde would slip its hand up your thigh. Where there would be no separation between desire and action because the avant-garde is desirable, sexy.

I want an avant-garde that can exist in everyday life, and not simply an avant-garde that uses everyday life. This is the difference between seeing someone move and knowing that she is performing Trio A versus being Yvonne Rainer and creating Trio A out of that moment. I want a world that is essentially avant-garde.

After all, we are now in a time of war, a time of the mineral-rich tragedies that form an avant-garde. We can look hungrily for a "nonmoral imperative," a drive to change things. My friend wrote me a letter explaining that he was searching for signs that there is a war. "The electricity went out last night," he wrote. "This makes sense because there is a war on."[*] And I am hoarding books like they were generators or PowerBars in hopes that I might stumble upon a mode of thinking that can formulate some belief in

---

[*] From Michael Cataldi's project, *Half Mast* (2006).

a belief in change. An artist recently told me that he thinks things are changing. He told me that this summer he participated in the Moscow Biennial, entitled "Dialectics of Hope," which he described as aiming to encourage people to rebelieve in belief. I see a similar trend in the Bedford-like popularity of Alain Badiou and his wild declarations of "truth." For me, belief is stirring behind the desk at the Institute for the Return of the Radical Imagination. As I drift off into a history of disruption and change, I write in my notebook, "All of my imaginary boyfriends are revolutionaries."

# QUESTIONS

**KEITH GESSEN:** Thank you. So we've thrown some terms out. We have the progressive versus the perennial versus the avant-garde. In painting we have the practical and impractical avant-garde. We also have Joe Gonzalez, an example of the—I'm not sure where he would fall. But, listening to you all talk about the practical avant-garde and the perennial novel, one could accuse you of a certain conservatism. In *n+1*, we've published only one work that I think was indisputably avant-garde, and that is Vladimir Sorokin's *The Norm*, which is from twenty years ago, translated from the Russian.* Does that make us conservative?

**MARK GREIF:** Do other people want to weigh in? This is your chance to denounce *n+1* publicly.

There are two questions here. One is about the danger of turning into or sounding like a cultural conservative if you make demands, as Dushko did, for the good rather than the interesting, or if you make

---

* *n+1* Issue One, Fall 2004.

demands, as I did, for a progressive avant-garde, rather than one which just came up with new and interesting stuff. Question two is about the work that we actually publish, and whether I was in fact saying that *n+1* has no interest in, or no business in publishing avant-garde work.

In response to the second question, because it's the easier one: one of the things about all discussions of the avant-garde is that, especially when they involve actual practitioners—working writers, working artists, and so forth—they can become incredibly frustrating for artists. Often it makes them angry, because the artist or writer is put in a singularly equivocal position. In order to become part of an avant-garde that lasts and that people recognize, you have to declare yourself part of an avant-garde—you have to actually go around and say, "I'm part of an avant-garde! My work is avant-garde!" You have to write a manifesto. And yet, there also have to be certain kinds of historical forces that align to legitimate your claim. If the historical forces are not working for you, people will just laugh you out of town when you get up and say, "I've started the neo-this, I'm part of an avant-garde." At other times, they will believe you. I think what I was arguing for was something on the side of historical circumstances, and the ability to identify them and to create institutional settings to evaluate them, like *n+1*, and like its "Symposium on American Writing" in

Issue Four, which I suggest you purchase and recommend to your family.

The real answer, I think, is rather than me saying, "Stop your avant-garde practice and start doing progressive work!"—which would be hard to do anyway, because only before the bar of history does a lot of art become meaningful and progressive—I'm saying people should be doing the work that's in their hearts, and which they find to be life and death for them. And yet, if you're sitting and writing about this stuff, or talking about it, or publishing a magazine, I think it's your job to try to figure out where this work that's coming in through the mail actually fits into the situation of your life, and everybody's life, and history. As for the conservative thing, it's true that there was a point while I was preparing my talk when I came across old material from the *New Criterion* from 1982—a journal I don't care for. Yet the *New Criterion* seemed to be defending the great works of modernism against a spurious avant-garde as well. And I was filled with horror, of course, because I thought we might in some way be echoing these kinds of claims. And certainly, I think it matters that we were brought up in an era marked by a refusal of hierarchies and a recognition that strong distinctions were only made by tyrants and cultural commissars. This was the kind of schooling I had. The great heroes were people who held spontaneous Beat poetry readings, during which they would chant, and ideally not record what they were doing, though of course they did record it, which is why you can still see Beat films and a bearded Allen Ginsberg on DVD. It's very odd to be in a position of declaring for what sound like *criteria* again, but maybe that's something we have to confront.

**DUSHKO PETROVICH:** I'd just add that the other way I can always identify a conservative is if someone doesn't like anything, or very, very little. Conservatives say things are bad, but they'll say it *a lot*. It's a question of ratios. The people sitting up here are also very enthusiastic about certain things, and not in a conservative way.

**GESSEN:** Conservatives also use the word "derivative" a lot, to pretend like something has already happened. I have another question–

**GREIF:** Uh, Keith, there's a question back there. A real person's question.

**MEGHAN O'ROURKE:** Thank you guys for your talks. From an artist's point of view today, why does it matter to us to have an avant-garde? We understand why, from a critic's point of view, you would want the avant-garde. It's part of the discussion, as Mark was saying, to try to derive different definitions, and delineate trends within the scene at large. I'm both a poet and an editor. It makes sense that the avant-garde of the late 19th and early 20th centuries was important because it was in reaction to a unified art world that had rules and ramifications. At this moment in time, certainly in poetry, there is more plurality than ever. Why would you want an avant-garde? The avant-gardes are in some way always tyrannical—the surrealists, fighting with the Dadaists, and so forth.

**PETROVICH:** If you have a very monolithic situation, or, as Mark alluded to, if you have an academy which is extremely strong and rigid, excluding a lot of things, or a way of thinking which is monolithic and actually has cultural power, then that kind of historical avant-garde is incredibly necessary. You have to go in—it's like a military history thing—and actually break up the ranks in order for there to be any space in which anyone can do something. But that situation in no way resembles the situation now. If we are grateful for the freedom and openness that we have as creative people now, I think we can be grateful to the previous avant-gardes. But, as Mark did a good job of pointing out, the nature or existence of the avant-garde depends a lot on the immediate historical situation.

**NEWMAN-SAUL:** The importance of the "avant-garde" as a term isn't as relevant as the need for a place for radical thinking to exist, and a way and system that supports that radical thinking. Art has historically been a place, poetry has historically been a place, where there is room for the extreme, for extremes of thought and extremes of presentation of the self, in art objects. Whether that is avant-garde or not is not as pressing as the importance of taking seriously this thing which must exist in the world, for these people. I think that is why art remains exciting. And what it has to offer is the room to take on these bold moments which the avant-garde took on, and that will continue.

**GREIF:** To follow up on Eliza's talk, too, I was reminded that one of the major functions of the avant-garde is to contribute to the imaginative erotic life of teenagers. That's very important. Specifically, to make you believe that in fact the adult world is going to be better than what you're living in now, rather than that childhood itself is the best period of your life. For the question of poetry and the literary arts, in particular, it has to be said that the minimal defense of the avant-garde for its own sake, which you always have to make, is that, whatever you believe are its immediate consequences, it's only by the ceaseless production of the absolutely new in formal terms—as formal resources—by novelists and poets of the avant-garde, that anybody else can figure out how these things work more constructively and synthetically. There's no James Joyce without a whole bunch of forgotten French writers.

**ANTHONY SMITH:** I was wondering whether you guys could speak to the larger cultural forces that might explain why we don't have a very interesting avant-garde right now. It occurred to me that, perhaps, if one can say there are a whole lot of boring artists out there, I wonder, is that because there's no cultural court pressing people at large to create something interesting and new? Eliza mentioned the war. This is a war in which nothing seems really to be challenging us enough to lead to the creation of an authentic and significant avant-garde. Instead we have artists who are replicating themselves, who are self-obsessed.

**MARCO ROTH** [co-editor of *n+1*]: Can I say something? Listening to these talks, I felt there was an elephant in the room. And it's a political elephant. I don't need to name the elephant, do I?

**GREIF:** Name the elephant.

**ROTH:** It's our political situation. I was struck by something in Mark's talk about the weightlessness of the avant-garde. There's an analogy with the contemporary left. The left fights with itself; it's without direction. There's a sense that we have movements that are

anti-imperialist or anti-globalist. There's a Progressive
Party, there's a progressive wing of the Democratic
Party, we don't know what the Democratic Party is.
Traditionally, there's been an avant-garde that works
to separate art from politics entirely, but then there's
also been an avant-garde that stands for linking aesthetic practice to politics and even basing aesthetic
practice on politics. Our generation has become suspicious of this because we've seen, as the first ques-
tioner said, that avant-gardes can be tyrannical; they
can be allied to tyrannical regimes. But we don't really
know yet what can come after that knowledge. The
question is: Is there a way we can begin a workshop
or research movement toward a progressive—even an
avant-garde-progressive—alliance of aesthetics with
politics that does not repeat the mistakes that were
made in the '20s and the '30s and does not end up in
atomization or weightless gestures of protest? It's OK
to have political art now, because art has been so suc-
cessfully separated from the spheres of everyday life
and practice in this country that there seems to be no
way back. This, to some degree, is the cultural moment
we find ourselves in now. If we had solutions to this,
we'd be here offering solutions. Instead we have questions. It's important to name the moment that we're in
and even to ask whether the effort of a political art is
worth it—without drawing this commissar list of what
a politically correct aesthetic practice would be; that's

not what we want. In *n+1*, we try to publish things that open up aesthetic and political questions quite explicitly. This is our ongoing moment of research. We hope this will fire someone's imagination and open things up to more work. We can't repeat the mistakes of the past, but we shouldn't just say, "We can't repeat the mistakes of the past, or we'll all become Stalinists again." The left has gone down this road before, and it's done nothing.

**GESSEN:** Amen. I actually wanted to throw the question about poetry back to Meghan. Will you stand up again? It seems like poetry has a very clear avant-garde—or for me, from the outside, I feel as if I can define what the avant-garde is for poetry, more clearly. Right?

**O'ROURKE:** I guess.

**GESSEN:** Well, how do you feel about it?

**O'ROURKE:** I actually would say—this is to generalize completely—but I don't think there's really an avant-garde in poetry. Avant-garde has itself become the norm. There is, no doubt, poetry that's truly avant-garde, but there's also a lot of what's called experimental, or "elliptical" poetry, a name that Stephen Burt gave to it. It rides on the coattails of Apollinaire, in the belief that all language is poetic—an initial avant-garde poetic doctrine which made it to America. A lot of the poetry that I see would fall under the category of avant-garde, but it's self-consciously avant-gard*ish*. It doesn't necessarily correspond to any degree of actual innovation or radical imagination, the term that Eliza used. For poetry, I would like the term radical imagination a lot more right now than I like the word avant-garde, because I think there's a lot of "avant-garde" poetry that's actually quite conventional.

**GESSEN:** One of the questions this raises for me is that, in poetry, there's a series of formal innovations; in painting, the same sort of thing. I feel like for the novel, formal innovations are much less interesting than are innovations in subject matter and narrative technique. What we mostly see as innovations are typographical things; those are more recognizable. What about painting, Dushko? Is there a way to move forward in subject matter or in things that are not strictly technical?

**PETROVICH:** Yes, the question of subject matter is always open. In terms of our cultural situation, we were in one mode, and then, not to be clichéd about it, but 9/11 was a watershed, and maybe it should have been an even bigger watershed for the national consciousness and then for the artistic one. I'm always shocked at how little art is actually being made directly about

the war. I wrote a little bit about Steve Mumford* precisely because he seemed to be one of the only people
who was taking it on, whether you liked what he did or
not. It was admirable to take it on. I think a lot of the
problem actually is a—I don't know what to call it—a
kind of a daydream of the American left. Artistically,
at this moment in history, we have to be practical.
We've been subjected to a dipshit President, and we're
not even the ones who are suffering the most from
his regime. The people in this room are insulated to
a large extent from the real devastation of his programs. Maybe when the artistic class starts to really
get affected, it'll start to make work which responds
to these situations. But so far I think the cultural tone
from before 9/11 has predominated, and I just can't
believe that.

**IRIS BERNBLUM:** I just had a question about the idea
of a radical imagination. I can't see what the point of
it is. I don't understand your definition of radical. So I
wondered if you could define it.

**NEWMAN-SAUL:** Being brought up in a postmodern
culture, we are taught not to believe in anything, and I
am interested in reasserting a certain type of ability to

---

* Steve Mumford is a New York City artist who, in 2003, spent time
painting, sketching, and photographing his experience as a combat
artist embedded in the Army's Third Infantry Division in Iraq.

imagine. And that imagination is—maybe not a solution per se, but a movement toward solution. It is my idea that we are in an age of research. We are in an age of thinking, of reading, of processing, and this is the most radical thing I can think of doing right now. Being active in a customary way—being an activist and standing in space—doesn't make you exist any more than you do in thinking. The specifics of my thoughts are not what is radical, but what is radical is the need to think. The ability to disassociate—not as the solution, but as an important part of a process.

**JAMES SUROWIECKI:** I have two questions, and they sort of flow together. The first is, does the avant-garde need to be marginal? In other words, if you become successful, can you still be part of the avant-garde? I guess when I try to think about truly successful art, or the art that moves me most, it feels like art that is walking a line between radical innovation, either in form or content, and a striving to hit themes or reach an audience that's bigger. Obviously, there are older avant-gardes that now qualify as an establishment. But today, can you be a successful artist, even a commercially successful artist for that matter, and still be considered avant-garde?

And then the second question flows out of that one, and that is, what about the question of pleasure, or fun, or enjoyment? The enjoyment of an avant-garde work by the audience? Because I think in a lot of people's minds, avant-garde work—especially contemporary avant-garde work—is associated with . . . well, fun is not the first word that comes to mind. Or pleasure, in a rich sense. Ben Marcus's piece in *Harper's\** is a somewhat strange piece, but a lot of it is about the sense that labor was really involved in what it meant to consume an avant-garde work. Mark, you didn't mention film, but I was thinking about film, and thinking about Michael Snow, or a lot of the avant-garde work of the '60s. It's hard to watch. Or *Empire*—*Empire*'s a great idea; it's hard to watch it for eight hours.\*\* I think there's a connection between the question of marginality and the question of pleasure.

**GREIF:** Two quick things for two questions—or maybe three quick things for two questions, I don't know, we'll see how it works. On the question of whether avant-garde art has to stay marginal, especially economically marginal, to function: I think rather than say anything of my own, I have to turn to Pierre Bourdieu. He said

---

\* Ben Marcus, "Why Experimental Fiction Threatens to Destroy Publishing, Jonathan Franzen, and Life As We Know It: A Correction." *Harper's* , October 2005.

\*\* *Empire* is Andy Warhol's 1964 film which consists of one stationary shot of the Empire State Building, in 16 mm without sound, and lasting approximately eight hours.

everything right out straight. He said, the world of art is dominated by particular norms, as is the rest of the world. The magical thing about the world of art is that, even though it is close to the dominating portion of society, that is, the world of people who have money, the poles are reversed in the artistic sphere so that only those people who are able to *avoid* money and refuse money for long enough are ever able to have any stature. Specifically, only they come to have the power to declare, "I am an artist," and to declare that other people are artists.

**GESSEN:** For which eventually they will be paid a lot of money.

**GREIF:** Yes, and so it's essentially a game of loser wins, where only if you are able to keep away from money long enough, will you eventually be rewarded with prizes and credentials, and be able to credential other people. And yet, if you don't, during the period when you're staying away from money, maintain in the back of your mind these economic norms in order to finesse them, you'll actually fall so far outside of art that you'll cease to make objects which function in its system, you'll no longer be counted as an artist, and you'll just be wiped out. Right? One of the crucial things about many of the art movements that Dushko was describing—which I wish I had the name for . . . Who's the guy who got nailed to the Volkswagen?

**PETROVICH:** Chris Burden.

**GREIF:** Right, Chris Burden. One of the crucial things about these people is that they have their actions recorded. And yet, really, an aspect of the long avant-garde tradition, from Dada and so forth, is a kind of negativism, an anti-art process, the destruction of art. A person who truly believed those precepts would not record any of his actions or tell anyone about them. I mean, *that* would be genuinely anti-art. And yet, were you to undertake that, you would be removed from the artistic system, and never gain any of the legitimating force associated with art, never gain museum power.

That said, I've argued elsewhere that, in fact, it often seems that the works that are most powerful at what it is I am asking art to do—really to capture the things in your life you find it most hard to articulate—are slightly withdrawn from the technical avant-garde. I argued this in my piece on Radiohead.* I know it sounds frivolous. But part of my argument is that, in pop music, it's often the case that the most avant-garde people are very advanced electronic artists, making remarkable music. You listen to their work, and you're

---

* *n+1* Issue Three, Fall 2005.

in a new age. No one in the history of humanity before this has ever heard 350 beats per minute. When you listen to it, part of the appeal is the patina of technicality. And yet, there are other musicians who are more withdrawn from the edge, but when you listen to their stuff, which integrates the technical methods often in a cruder and simpler and less advanced way, you say—*that*'s what my life sounds like. That's what the airport sounds like, or the highway.

On the question of "fun," I just think that the word has been so sterilized, by use and misuse, that we're at a philistine point, you know—"when I hear the word fun I reach for my revolver." This is a problem with that Ben Marcus essay, which may or may not be worth talking about, frankly. Isn't there a profounder pleasure in using experimental language to discover new capabilities of real depiction, or representation, rather than this aimlessness of building your "reading muscles," or game playing, or special pleading for happenstance alternate routes to fun? When I hear Radiohead and hear the world I'm living in, that qualifies as the affect or emotion I want, rather than fun.

GESSEN: I think the Marcus essay is interesting, because another person who represents this complex situation is Jonathan Franzen, in *The Corrections*, whom Marcus criticizes. Here is someone who was describing a certain historical situation of five years ago, and doing so in a way that I thought nobody had. Reading him, I was very conscious of the tradition that he was working in, of avant-garde writers, or more difficult writers, and yet his book was different. And then, immediately, he began to express his anxiety in public—especially when he was picked for Oprah—that he had somehow betrayed his tradition, and he was very worried about where this led him. So, as the Marcus thing captured, it led him to write a few things that I wish he hadn't written. Franzen attacked William Gaddis, for example, and said something like "Well you can only push a novel so far before it becomes unreadable," sort of defending the method of *The Corrections*. So Marcus seems to be arguing against a person who is already very worried about this, and has already made this argument himself, and against himself. Part of the trouble for me with the Marcus thing is that he seemed to present experimental work as if it were just a different flavor of ice cream, and not a means for getting at truth, which struck me as a sort of empty avant-garde.

**CHRISTIAN LORENTZEN:** I would like to direct a question toward Mark and Keith. Dushko mentioned careerism pejoratively. But it seemed right to me that he would call it, even jokingly, the major movement of the last century. Isn't that in a way preferable—for a situation in which an artist's biography tends to climax in tenure rather than suicide? That's my question for Mark and Keith.

**GREIF:** Tenure or suicide?

**LORENTZEN:** Precisely. What are the possibilities, and then, what are the drawbacks?

**GESSEN:** What about adjunct status or suicide?

**LORENTZEN:** Then, I would say, isn't the act of starting a magazine, as you guys have, a hyper-careerist act in and of itself? Therefore, yes, I guess I am accusing you of careerism and asking you to either defend yourselves or plead guilty.

**PETROVICH:** I'd like to clarify my position. I think careerism is fine. It's too bad when it's a major movement, when it's so palpable, you know what I mean? It's like good-looking people putting on too much makeup. People should relax a little bit. They should be confident that they can make an art object on their own, without any credentials, any school, building, any of that stuff.

**GESSEN:** I'd define careerism as trying to advance yourself in existing institutions, whereas creating new institutions seems to be entering into a dialogue with pre-existing institutions.

**GREIF:** There are two questions, right? One is tenure versus suicide. The other is careerism. I do think that when artists kill themselves it's probably because of some problem in their personal lives rather than the recognition that it's the only way to keep themselves pure for their art. So it's not much of a choice. Now, to the question of whether starting a magazine qualifies as careerism. I remember through my childhood, at least through the teenage years, I was aware of the fact that, supposedly, e.e. cummings had had his very first book published by his mom. And in dark times, I used to think—if it comes to it, I'll have written this work, and . . . I will ask my mother. It will be published by my mom. And there'll be no shame in it because that's what e.e. cummings did.

**GESSEN:** But then it turned out that e.e. cummings' mother was the president of Random House.

**GREIF:** The bottom line is you write something, and you really believe in what you have to say. Of course, you write book reviews first because people will publish your book reviews. And then you write something else, something real, and you try to publish it. No way. There are many possible reactions to being left with these thoughts you can't get aired. One is becoming intimate with the publishing industry, modifying yourself. Another is giving up. If you decide you won't do either one, then you can do anything. Starting a magazine—why not? You believe in the stuff you wrote, and you really must publish it because you believe so much in this stuff. The world must know! About Radiohead! Of course, the more altruistic aspect is that you probably know a lot of people who are also not being published as they should be, and that is the only rationale really for *n+1.*

**NIKIL SAVAL:** My question is about the university. You brought up the point that the university is not just a place for the artist to reside, but also a place that regulates and distributes the very terms that get adopted in this dialogue. I'm worried about any description of an avant-garde that requires the university as an institutional safe haven. I think, I guess I fear, that this word "radical," for example, is now most at home in a university situation and most at home in university journals. I understand that *n+1* is in dialogue with the university, but it would be specious to believe that it doesn't also depend on it. So what place for language, and what place for art?

**GESSEN:** I would first establish a fact. All poets right now are university poets and almost all working novelists, with some exceptions among very successful novelists, are in universities, and a lot of painters are in universities. So it's almost as if the radical poets and the traditional poets are all, with everybody, in the university. So, in a way, that makes the question more difficult. It also leads to the question, now that the English departments are turning into more pre-professional places and including creative writing divisions, of whether the institutions that supported and canonized radical works, the departments of criticism and scholarship, will still exist in thirty or forty years.

**GREIF:** Keith and I, and all of us, debate this question all the time—what is the role of the university? I feel a little differently from Keith about the assurance that all the poets are safely in English departments. I also think that of all the questions about art and writing in the second half of the 20th century, the toughest and most important one turns out to be about universitization. More and more, I'd suggest that we just don't have enough data. If there were truly talented sociologists or a team of them, perhaps even as many as 100, who would actually administer questionnaires about working habits and salaries and perhaps even sit down and audit the time of these writers, then I think we would finally know what we need to know. So much of what is said about universitization depends on a level of rumor, and on amazing overgeneralizations about what happens to the artist when he enters the university.

The other thing that you asked about, though, was not so much about the question of artists in the university or writers in the university, but about the university's teaching of avant-garde terms, or not even avant-garde terms but *aesthetic* terms, which include the avant-garde itself and certain measures and tests of the avant-garde. It is true that this would not have been the case during, oh, World War II, but certainly it's solidly in the curriculum by the '60s and '70s and '80s, and after that when we were all in school. There's the sense that you can go to a class on surrealism and be instructed on all the various movements and the necessary steps—you know, "Take a revolver into a theater; that would be avant-garde." So when you talk about the institutional capture of even the words with which we mean to describe art which would somehow stand outside of the institution—and certainly when the people in the 1970s and 1980s who found that they had been deprived of NEA funding kept turning to, you know, the Wexner Center [at Ohio State University] or other university places to get the funding to make art that was supposedly "subversive"—you do get a little problem. Maybe that wasn't your question.

**SAM FRANK:** I'd just like you to name some names. I'm finding this discussion a little infuriating because it is just too ungrounded. Dushko, I went along with a lot of what you said, but in the end you're saying, we should keep what's good and reject what's bad. I'd like you to name some artists who are doing that. With the "radical imagination"—who has radical imagination? At the other end of the table, *n+1*, it seems like you've been engaged—you know, you've written about France and Radiohead, you've written about Woody Allen and Wes Anderson and Philip Roth—it seems like your engagement is not with anything one would call avant-garde. It's intelligent, it's middlebrow—it's middlebrow the way the *New Yorker* is a high-quality middlebrow magazine, and *n+1* wants to be a higher-quality middlebrow magazine, maybe. Are you engaged at all with the avant-garde (which you, um, claim to be)? And who could you like in the avant-garde?

**PETROVICH:** I like, for example, Neo Rausch. He's a very good painter. You want me just to name names?

**FRANK:** Well, yeah. Do your best.

**PETROVICH:** What I think the situation of painting is now, or the most interesting painting for me, is that it looks back on all the technical advances and experimentation that went on in the last century. I think the last century has been an incredibly experimental century, right? And I think, now, so many of those endgames have been played out to the point where you can literally put anything on the surface of a painting, whether it be paint or sand or feces or urine or blood, or, you know, you name it. Plastic, hot oil . . . Anyway, what the most interesting people do is take all that, and then they apply it to our current situation and our current consciousness, and they produce pictures that are compelling. I think that's actually an enormous project. So I like Neo Rausch, I like Amy Sillman, I like a young painter called Chie Fueki. We did a piece on a painter I admire, Steve Mumford. I admire Marvin Gates—do you want more? I don't know if these people constitute an actual avant-garde, which is why I invented the term "practical avant-garde," which I think is a boring term that I use to deliver what my values are within painting. Roger White, who is in the audience, is another painter I admire.

**NEWMAN-SAUL:** Artists that I would say have a "radical imagination"? I don't think it's particularly limited to art per se. I think it comes on with a certain separation or pain. But I think that Thomas Hirschhorn is a really interesting artist, I think that Barrett Watten's *Bad History* is a really interesting book, I think Sophie Calle is really interesting. I wouldn't limit it to art. I think there are some really interesting chefs. I think it's a much broader term than simply a term for art.

**GESSEN:** I mentioned that we published Sorokin in the first issue, we published Alexander Kluge in the second issue, we're publishing Grégoire Bouillier in Issue Four—which leads me to think that these people all come from other countries. You know, this fiction portfolio that we're doing this issue—it's four pieces, one of which has been described by one of our interns as "pretentious near-nonsense," thus locating it on this continuum of the avant-garde. There's a piece in it by John Haskell which we think deals with consciousness in a way that alters the surface of traditional narrative, in a way that's very interesting. I think some of these things we defend because no one else will defend them, not in a magazine like ours. There do exist places, like *Third Bed*, that are just born to publish stories which are not quite comprehensible, but stories that are clearly in this very tradition, in "the avant-garde." We don't feel that it's our place to do that, exactly.

**GREIF:** I just want to say, as strongly as possible, that I feel it is the job and the mission of *n+1* to be a *low*-quality *high*brow publication. You misunderstand what the middlebrow is.

**GESSEN:** We should say, the person who asked that question, Sam Frank, copyedited all four issues. So he does know whereof he speaks.

**LORETTA STAPLES:** I'm not exactly sure what my question is, but I guess I find myself here, um, wondering why you're talking about things in the way that you are. You talk very specifically about certain cultural genres—painting, poetry, writing. But some things that I think have been very powerful influences for me in the last several decades are computing, the digital, and design. And someone made a very offhand comment, "Oh, that's just typography," or something like that. I want you to know that I hate the digital and I hate designing, so I don't want you to think that I'm arguing on their behalf. But I feel like, in terms of factors that have very much influenced cultural production over the last two decades, those two things are major factors that you haven't really touched upon, and I think one of the things that I detect in a lot of contemporary art, and I would say in a lot of contemporary painting, is that it's all design. The fact that it is design is what is so, sort of, *bad* in the current state of affairs. Because people are turning to design to do things without knowing that that's what they're doing. I think this goes to Dushko's larger question about careerism, the problem of the field. It's like: "Oh yeah, I'm a painter, and I, like, build websites during the day." The digital has made everything this mushy playground, where actually, the discursive lines that would help shape the critical discourse just aren't there anymore, and that's why we have such a floppy situation. I think it's floppy, but it's oftentimes wonderful because, you know, there are people blogging and making digital photo albums—stuff that you would probably consider avant-garde—but they're just not in your sphere. They're not in your literary, artistic sphere, you know, they're like in Towanda, Kansas, blogging.

**PETROVICH:** I think it's a very good question. I'll just speak to this question of "designed" paintings. One of the things that comes up a lot right now in the art world is this word "interdisciplinary," which is a buzzword. I think it's odd. My favorite interdisciplinary artist was Michelangelo, and he was really good at architecture, and sculpture, and painting—and probably in that order. William Blake was another good interdisciplinary artist. I think interdisciplinary art has been going on for a long time. Sometimes, it's used as a cover for a noncommittal attitude, and I think that's actually a problem. Loretta said it very well when she said that paintings get designed. Design is great for a tennis shoe, something where you have to know how it's built beforehand, but I think there are other forms of art for which you wouldn't want to have the ideas totally worked out beforehand. Painting usually falls into the second category. In terms of the discursive lines, my way of looking at it is always that one should have a level of, I don't know if you'd call it expertise, or discipline, before one's work can become interdisciplinary. I'm a painter who writes criticism, and those are two disciplines. I try to practice them both, but I wouldn't want to reach a point where I was collaging them or putting the works of other painters into my work in that way. In terms of the digital, I mean . . . we have a website. In one of our pieces we talked about how Steve Mumford had taken watercolors and scanned them in and put them on a website, and how that was different from seeing watercolors in the flesh, and how there's a machine that's operating. I'm dying to write an essay called "The Work of Art in the Age of Digital Reproduction" because I think that's a major, major issue—but it's not going to come out in the next ten minutes.

**NEWMAN-SAUL:** I think that the design question becomes the means by which a lot of artists who are not interested in ideas are following through and thinking about what they're doing. The most important thing that you can teach in art is how to think about an idea. It isn't really taught in the universities. I think a lot of people come into art because they were told they drew well in high school. They get into an art world that expects ideas and expects you to be articulate and expects you to be innovative and—I think it's really overwhelming for a lot of people. Design is one way to think through those problems, or problems as such.

**GREIF:** Do people in the audience want to follow up with questions about design, or do I get to talk about community access television?

**PETROVICH:** Do it.

**GREIF:** Community access television! I, too, find that when I talk enough about painting and literature, it does make me want to stop talking about them, and start talking about television and food. Those two have much more to do with my life than anything (well, except for literature). I did have the experience recently of going to see the reinstalled Museum of Modern Art. I don't live in New York. It was very exciting for me, and, of course, there is much more video art than there was before, and it's now at the center of the collection. I saw all the video art at the new MoMA, and then I went home and—you see, the really great thing about New York is that, at night, you can watch community access cable television. There are at least four stations. And something became clear.

I often feel that video art is one of the great artistic disappointments of the second half of the 20th century, because, in fact, you would think it would be the best of all artistic media and all genres. It is often argued that people today are becoming less and less literate, which seems largely true, but they are certainly becoming more televisually literate. And so you would imagine that the great bulk of people in the first world, having been deprived of words, would be so saturated with images—and moreover, with a consciousness that can accept such an extraordinary quantity of images and reproduce them—that these people would produce extraordinary works on video, just by sheer putting together of images.

There is a kind of history of what happened to video art that explains why you don't see that kind of genius, namely that, for museum presentation, people who were already artists in other media, but would then film their own hands, heads, bodies, in their studios, on video, wound up in the museum. But many of the people who worked more in the critique of television, simply by, for example, intercutting television events, often wound up in other places, like community access cable. So now if you turn on community access cable late at night, you can see that there's a show called *Concrete TV*. I try to find it whenever I'm in town—if I *can* find it (it's on at 2 AM). The title comes from *musique concrète*, I guess. It's just thousands upon thousands of edited television shows that this video editor keeps at home, in which you see not one car crash, not two car crashes, but five or twenty car crashes all in a row, and, moreover, car crashes which often occupy the same visual space within the frame of the television. You learn from this not so much about art, but about television, and you really learn something deep. Whenever I watch it, even though the thing is meant for thrills—you're watching people kicking each other in the face, cars crashing—in fact I find I'm possessed by a deep calm. It's the same calm that, on a smaller scale, is the calm of watching television generally, because of its endless repetition. This is the fundamental structure of television: repetition. I think *Concrete TV* is better than just about anything in the MoMA video art display, a work of genius. And I think it's very often going to be the case that, in this sense, the most avant-garde work, the most revealing work, is going to be found—insofar as our lives are dominated by design—*in* design, although maybe only on the fringes of it, and—insofar as our lives are dominated by television—*on* television, though, again, on the fringes.

**ROBIN KIRMAN:** I'm just wondering why you think in terms of the avant-garde rather than something more general, like "movement." Does the avant-garde always include something like a teleology, a discussion of whether one movement is better than another, more generative than others, and therefore more useful for us? Should we go around picking and choosing one movement as more useful than another, or should we just have . . . movement?

**GREIF:** I think the right approach to the value of the avant-garde is that, above all, it declares in favor of formal novelty—for better and for worse. Avant-gardists are the only people guaranteed to feel an impulse to develop new formal resources.

**GESSEN:** I didn't know you thought that.

**GREIF:** Yes, I do.

**PETROVICH:** I just have scattered thoughts. Looking at that word "radical," and looking at the title *n+1*, and thinking about the word "progressive," all these things contain the notion of a direction. That's the best thing a movement can provide. But the reason I'm always cheeky about movements or disappointed in them is that usually they end up deteriorating into a marketable, recognizable brand rather than any kind of genuine direction. I'm also very suspicious of groups of artists, because there's a way in which a hierarchy emerges, things get codified, and the earliest ideas get kicked out. I think the surrealists are a really great example. Joseph Brodsky used to say that classicism and Greek mythology were good surrealism—and later it became something kind of silly. Picasso is probably the best surrealist, and he got kicked out. Those are my thoughts about that.

**POLYANNA RHEE:** Mark mentioned the Wexner Center, and I've been thinking about architecture. It's not clear to me how architects would go about an avant-garde investigation because often, in architecture, you're just doing all this crazy shit when you're in school, and then when you get out, you do bathroom details for a Barnes & Noble store. You can't be assured that your "formal investigations" have any meaning. So, someone like Peter Eisenman wrote all this crazy shit, and when he was in his fifties, finally built his D-Con building*, which is actually pretty bad—

**PETROVICH:** Yeah.

**RHEE:** —but it's good as an idea that was built. It started people thinking more about how architecture could be more substantive, ideas versus matter, outside of just paper. So can't the bad start something that's ultimately productive?

---

* Peter Eisenman's Greater Columbus Convention Center in Columbus, Ohio, 1990-1993.

**GESSEN:** Aha! That would be the impractical avant-garde.

**PETROVICH:** I'm from Columbus, so I've experienced that building. I think that building is kind of an impractical building. I like the way it looks. And I like the *idea* of an idea generating something. But, what I want to say, and what I guess I said in my speech, is: you can start with a good idea, but in the end you have to deliver something that exists in the world. Between those two poles, the best people are whoever can make it from point A to B, and they can be radical all along—Eliza and I were talking about this earlier. It doesn't necessarily matter so much what you do in your preparatory time to get there, but we do need to require a certain kind of *effectiveness*, in the end, from people in the various arts.

**COLBY CHAMBERLAIN** [P.S.1 programming coordinator]: Let's wrap things up there, and move it over to the café. Thank you all for coming.

*This discussion took place at P.S.1 Contemporary Art Center on March 18, 2006 before an audience of 200.*